Our Favorite Pumpkin Recipes

Copyright 2019, Gooseberry Patch

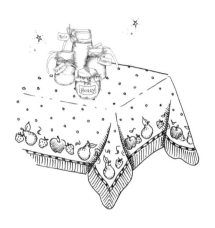

Colorful oilcloth is so pretty as a table covering
and has the added bonus of being quick & easy
to clean. Ideal when breakfast calls for
sticky syrup or honey!

Chocolate Chip-Pumpkin Waffles

Serves 4

1 egg, beaten
3/4 c. canned pumpkin
1/4 c. brown sugar, packed
1/4 c. butter, melted and
    slightly cooled
1-3/4 c. milk
1-1/2 c. all-purpose flour
1/2 c. whole-wheat flour

1 T. flax meal
1-1/2 t. pumpkin pie spice
1 T. baking powder
1/2 t. salt
1/2 c. semi-sweet chocolate chips
Optional: vanilla yogurt,
    cinnamon-sugar, toasted
    pumpkin seeds

In a bowl, whisk together egg, pumpkin, brown sugar, butter and milk. Add flours, flax meal, spice, baking powder and salt; whisk well until smooth. Fold in chocolate chips. Pour batter by 1/2 cupfuls into a greased hot waffle iron. Cook waffles according to manufacturer's directions. Top waffles with a dollop of yogurt, cinnamon-sugar and pumpkin seeds, if desired.

Sprinkle a little pumpkin pie spice over dollops
of whipped cream...yummy on servings of
pancakes, French toast or waffles.

Make-Ahead Pumpkin Pie French Toast

Serves 8

1 loaf French, Italian, challah
   or Hawaiian bread, cut into
   1-inch slices
3 eggs, beaten
1/2 c. egg substitute
1 c. half-and-half
1-1/2 c. milk
1/4 t. salt
1 t. vanilla extract
1 T. pumpkin pie spice
1/2 c. brown sugar, packed
1 to 2 T. butter, sliced

Arrange bread slices in the bottom of a greased 13"x9" baking pan. Whisk together eggs, egg substitute, half-and-half, milk, salt, vanilla and spice. Stir in brown sugar; pour mixture over bread slices. Refrigerate, covered, overnight. Dot top with butter and bake, uncovered, at 350 degrees for 40 to 45 minutes.

Set the breakfast table the night before...
enjoy a relaxed breakfast in the morning!

Pumpkin Pie Oatmeal

Serves 4

4 c. water
2 c. old-fashioned oats, uncooked
1/8 t. salt
1 c. canned pumpkin
1/2 c. brown sugar, packed

1 t. pumpkin pie spice
Optional: 1/2 c. chopped walnuts
or pecans, 1/2 c. golden
raisins
Garnish: milk or cream

Bring water to a boil in a medium saucepan over high heat. Stir in oats and salt; reduce heat to low. Simmer for about 10 minutes. Stir in pumpkin, brown sugar and spice; simmer another 5 minutes. Just before serving, stir in nuts or raisins, if desired. Serve warm with a splash of milk or cream.

Breakfast sliders! Whip up your favorite pancake batter
and make silver dollar–size pancakes. Sandwich them
together with slices of heat & serve sausage.
Serve with maple syrup on the side for dipping...yum!

Silver Dollar Pumpkin Pancakes   *Makes about 5 dozen mini pancakes*

2 eggs
1 c. milk
1/2 c. canned pumpkin
1/4 c. canola oil
1-3/4 c. biscuit baking mix

2 T. sugar
1/2 t. ground ginger
1/2 t. cinnamon
1/2 t. nutmeg
Garnish: butter, pancake syrup

In a bowl, beat eggs with an electric mixer on high speed for 3 to 5 minutes, until thick and lemon-colored. Reduce speed to medium; beat in milk, pumpkin and oil. Add biscuit mix, sugar and spices; beat on low speed until well blended. Pour batter by tablespoonfuls onto a lightly greased griddle over medium heat. For full-size pancakes, pour batter by 1/4 to 1/2 cupfuls. Cook until puffy and bubbles begin to form around the edges. Turn and cook other side until golden. Serve pancakes garnished as desired.

Small-town county fairs, food festivals, swap meets...the list goes on & on, so grab a friend and go for good old-fashioned fun. A hearty warm breakfast will get you off to a terrific start.

Glazed Pumpkin Scones

Makes 8 scones

2 c. all-purpose flour
1/2 c. sugar
1 T. baking powder
1/2 t. salt
1-1/2 t. pumpkin pie spice

1/2 c. butter, diced
1/2 c. canned pumpkin
3 T. milk
1 egg, beaten

Combine flour, sugar, baking powder, salt and spice in a large bowl. Cut in butter with a pastry blender until crumbly; set aside. In a separate bowl, whisk together pumpkin, milk and egg. Fold pumpkin mixture into flour mixture. Form dough into a ball; pat out dough onto a floured surface. Form into a 9-inch circle. Cut into 8 wedges and place on a greased baking sheet. Bake at 425 degrees for 14 to 16 minutes. Drizzle scones with Powdered Sugar Glaze; allow to set.

Powdered Sugar Glaze:

1 c. powdered sugar
2 to 3 T. milk

1/2 t. pumpkin pie spice

Mix all ingredients together, adding enough milk for a drizzling consistency.

An easy and fun addition to your brunch table...
mini cinnamon buns! Start with a tube of refrigerated cinnamon
rolls; unroll the dough strips, cut in half lengthwise and sprinkle
with more cinnamon and sugar. Roll the strips into one-inch buns;
place in a well-greased mini muffin tin and bake as directed.
Allow to cool slightly; remove from tins while still warm.

Pumpkin Spice Coffee Cake

Serves 10 to 12

18-1/4 oz. pkg. spice cake mix
2 eggs, beaten
1/2 c. water
1/2 t. baking soda
15-oz. can pumpkin

8-oz. container frozen whipped
   topping, thawed
Garnish: cinnamon,
   nutmeg to taste

In a bowl, combine dry cake mix, eggs, water, baking soda and pumpkin. With an electric mixer on medium speed, beat for 2 minutes. Pour batter into 3 greased 8" round cake pans, or one greased 13"x9" baking pan. Bake at 350 degrees for 20 to 25 minutes, until a toothpick tests clean when inserted into cake's center. Allow to cool; spread with whipped topping and sprinkle with cinnamon and nutmeg. Cover and refrigerate.

Make a yummy ice cream sandwich with Sugary Pumpkin Doughnuts. Cut a doughnut in half and add a scoop of your favorite flavor ice cream between the two halves. Place on a baking sheet and freeze for one hour...tasty!

Sugary Pumpkin Doughnuts

Makes 2 to 3 dozen doughnuts

3-1/2 c. all-purpose flour
1 T. baking powder
1 t. baking soda
1 t. salt
1/2 t. cinnamon
1/2 t. ground ginger
1/4 c. butter, softened

1-1/4 c. sugar, divided
2 eggs
2/3 c. canned pumpkin
2/3 c. buttermilk
1/2 c. brown sugar, packed
oil for deep frying

In a bowl, sift together flour, baking powder, baking soda, salt and spices; set aside. In a separate large bowl, beat butter and 3/4 cup sugar with an electric mixer on medium speed until creamy. Add eggs, one at a time, beating well after each addition. Beat in 1/4 cup flour mixture; add pumpkin and buttermilk. Add remaining flour mixture; stir just until blended. Cover and refrigerate for 3 hours or overnight. Combine remaining sugar and brown sugar in a plastic bag; set aside. On a floured surface, roll dough to 1/3-inch thickness. Cut into doughnuts; let stand 10 minutes. Heat 1/2 inch oil to 360 degrees in a large skillet. Cook doughnuts on both sides until golden and cooked through, about 5 minutes. Place on paper towels to drain. While still warm, add each doughnut to bag with sugar; shake to coat.

A pint-size Mason jar filled with homemade fruit butter or
sweet spread makes a delightful (and yummy) gift to share
with co-workers and neighbors. Use a bit of jute or
raffia to tie on a pretty spreader.

Jill's Banana Butter

Makes 3 cups

4 ripe bananas, sliced
3 T. lemon juice

1-1/2 c. sugar
1 t. pumpkin pie spice

Place bananas and lemon juice in a food processor; pulse until smooth. Transfer mixture to a saucepan and stir in remaining ingredients. Bring to a boil over medium-high heat. Reduce heat to medium-low and simmer for 15 minutes, stirring often. Spoon into an airtight container; cover and keep refrigerated.

Put away summer toss pillows for the season...
set out warm & cozy cushions of flannel or fleece.

Maple-Pumpkin Butter

Makes 4 to 5 cups

3 c. canned pumpkin
1/2 c. brown sugar, packed
1/2 c. maple syrup
1/3 c. apple or pear juice

2 t. cinnamon
1/2 t. ground ginger
1/2 t. ground cloves

Combine all ingredients in a large saucepan over medium heat; bring to a simmer. Cook for 5 to 10 minutes, until well blended. Pour mixture into a 13"x9" baking pan sprayed with non-stick vegetable spray. Bake at 300 degrees for one hour and 15 minutes, stirring every 20 minutes, until thickened. Remove; cool slightly. Store in an airtight container; keep refrigerated for up to 4 weeks.

Greet family, friends and even passersby with pumpkin flowerpots. Fill plump, hollowed-out pumpkins with potted mums, then set on porch steps...sure to bring smiles.

Pumpkin Dip

Makes about 6 cups

2 8-oz. pkgs. cream cheese,
   softened
15-oz. can pumpkin
1/2 t. pumpkin pie spice

1/4 t. nutmeg
1/2 t. cinnamon
16-oz. pkg. powdered sugar
vanilla wafers, graham crackers

In a large bowl, beat cream cheese with an electric mixer on medium speed until smooth. Stir in pumpkin and spices; fold in powdered sugar. Cover and chill before serving. Serve with vanilla wafers or graham crackers.

Enter your preserves, jams, jellies or pickles in your local county fair. You just may be surprised at how well you do!

Nutty Pumpkin Butter

Makes 5 jars

3-1/2 c. canned pumpkin
1 c. pecans, toasted and chopped
1 T. pumpkin pie spice
1-3/4 oz. pkg. powdered pectin

1/2 t. butter
4-1/2 c. sugar
5 1/2-pint canning jars and lids, sterilized

Combine pumpkin, pecans and spice in a large saucepan; stir in pectin. Add butter and bring to a boil over high heat, stirring constantly. Quickly add sugar; stir to dissolve. Boil for one minute, stirring constantly. Remove from heat; skim off foam if needed. Spoon into hot sterilized jars, leaving 1/4-inch headspace. Wipe rims; secure lids and rings. Process in a boiling-water-bath for 15 minutes. Set jars on a towel to cool. Check for seals.

For the tenderest quick breads and muffins,
don't overmix...just stir the batter until moistened.
A few lumps won't matter.

Hazel's Pumpkin Bread

Makes 6 to 8 servings

1-2/3 c. all-purpose flour
1-1/4 c. sugar
1 t. baking soda
1/2 t. cinnamon
1/2 t. nutmeg
1/4 t. salt

1/2 c. oil
2 eggs, beaten
1 c. canned pumpkin
1/3 c. water
1/2 c. candied cherries, halved
1/2 c. chopped nuts

In a large bowl, combine flour, sugar, baking soda, spices and salt; set aside. In a separate bowl, whisk together oil, eggs, pumpkin and water. Add pumpkin mixture to flour mixture; mix well. Fold in cherries and nuts. Pour batter into a greased and floured 9"x5" loaf pan. Bake at 350 degrees for one hour, or until center tests done with a toothpick.

Hang an old-fashioned peg rack inside the back door, then hang up all the kids' backpacks plus a tote bag for yourself. Gather schoolbooks, permission slips, car keys and other important stuff before you go to bed. Less morning rush... more time to enjoy breakfast.

Pumpkin Biscotti

Serves 6 to 8

4 eggs, beaten
1 c. butter, melted and
    slightly cooled
1 t. vanilla extract
2 15.4-oz. pkgs. pumpkin muffin
    or quick bread mix

8-oz. pkg. white or milk chocolate
    chips, divided
1 to 3 T. all-purpose flour

In a large bowl, combine eggs, butter and vanilla; stir until well blended. Blend in dry muffin or quick bread mix and 1/2 cup chocolate chips; stir again. Mixture will be sticky. Add enough flour to form a smooth dough; knead on a lightly floured surface for several minutes. Divide dough in half; shape each half into an oval loaf and flatten slightly. Place on a lightly greased baking sheet. Bake at 350 degrees for 30 to 40 minutes, until golden. Remove from oven; set aside to cool for 15 to 20 minutes. Using a serrated knife, cut loaves into one-inch thick slices; arrange slices on baking sheet. Return to oven and continue to bake 15 minutes longer. Remove from oven; let cool. Melt remaining chocolate chips and drizzle over slices; cool.

Tuck votives inside Mason jars and set in the middle of urns
last used to hold summer's flowers. Surround the jars
with nuts, berries, hedge apples, gourds, mini pumpkins
and leaves...oh-so pretty.

Spiced Zucchini Bread

Makes one loaf

15.4-oz. pkg. nut bread mix
1 egg
1 t. pumpkin pie spice

2/3 c. milk
2 T. oil
1 c. zucchini, shredded

In a bowl, combine all ingredients except zucchini; mix until well blended. Fold in zucchini. Pour batter into a 9"x5" loaf pan that has been greased on the bottom only. Bake at 350 degrees for 45 to 55 minutes, until a toothpick inserted in the center comes out clean. Turn out loaf onto a wire rack; cool before slicing.

Practical and pretty napkin rings...twist lengths of
bittersweet into a circle, tucking in colorful leaves
and mums. They're so creative on your Fall dinner table!

Pumpkin Cornbread

Makes 9 servings

4 T. butter, divided
1 onion, finely chopped
1 c. yellow cornmeal
2/3 c. all-purpose flour
1 T. baking powder
1/2 t. baking soda

3/4 t. salt
1/4 t. pepper
1 c. canned pumpkin
2 T. honey
2 eggs, beaten
3/4 c. buttermilk

Heat one tablespoon butter in a non-stick skillet over medium heat. Sauté onion for 5 minutes, or until softened and golden. In a large bowl, combine cornmeal, flour, baking powder, baking soda, salt and pepper; set aside. In a separate bowl, stir together pumpkin, honey, eggs, buttermilk and onion mixture. Add remaining butter to a 9"x9" baking pan. Set pan in oven; bake at 400 degrees until butter is melted. Swirl pan to coat with butter. Pour melted butter into pumpkin mixture; stir to combine. Add pumpkin mixture to cornmeal mixture; stir just until moistened. Pour batter into pan; smooth top. Bake at 400 degrees for 25 to 30 minutes, until a toothpick inserted in center comes out clean. Cut into squares; serve warm.

O, it sets my heart a-clickin' like the tickin' of the clock,
When the frost is on the pumpkin and the fodder's in the shock.

–James Whitcomb Riley

Pumpkin-Chocolate Chip Muffins   *Makes one dozen*

1 c. canned pumpkin
1/2 c. brown sugar, packed
1/4 c. butter, melted and slightly
    cooled
2 eggs, beaten

2 c. all-purpose flour
2 t. baking powder
1/2 t. salt
1 c. semi-sweet chocolate chips

In a large bowl, mix together all ingredients in the order given. Spoon batter into 12 paper-lined muffin cups, filling about 3/4 full. Bake at 375 degrees for 20 minutes, or until muffins test done with a toothpick.

To create a fragrant pumpkin, use an apple corer to carve out round vents in a hollowed-out pumpkin. Rub pumpkin pie spice or cinnamon on the underside of the pumpkin's lid, or push cloves into it. Set a lighted tea-light candle inside. This will give off a delightful scent for about 6 hours.

Pumpkin Biscuits

Makes one to 1-1/2 dozen

2 c. all-purpose flour
4 T. sugar, divided
1 T. baking powder
1 t. baking soda
1/4 t. salt
1/4 t. cinnamon

1/4 t. nutmeg
1/4 t. allspice
1/2 c. butter
2/3 c. canned pumpkin
1/2 c. buttermilk

In a large bowl, sift together flour, 2 tablespoons sugar, baking powder, baking soda, salt and spices. Cut in butter until mixture resembles coarse crumbs; set aside. In a small bowl, whisk together pumpkin and buttermilk. Add to flour mixture and stir to combine. Knead dough gently a few times. On a floured surface, roll out dough to 1/2-inch thickness; cut out biscuits with a round biscuit or cookie cutter. Place biscuits on a lightly greased baking sheet; sprinkle tops with remaining sugar. Bake at 450 degrees for 10 minutes, or until lightly golden.

Need a gift in a jiffy for a teacher, a neighbor or
a friend with a new baby? Give a loaf of freshly baked
quick bread wrapped in a pretty tea towel...
it's sure to be appreciated.

Vanilla-Glazed Pumpkin Bread

Makes 3 mini loaves

4 eggs, beaten
3 c. sugar
15-oz. can pumpkin
3-1/2 c. all-purpose flour
1 t. baking powder
2 t. baking soda
2 t. salt

1 t. nutmeg
1/2 t. cinnamon
1 c. oil
2/3 c. water
3 t. vanilla extract
1 c. chopped pecans

Beat eggs and sugar in a large bowl until fluffy; add pumpkin and mix well.
In another bowl, combine flour, baking powder, baking soda, salt and spices.
Stir flour mixture into egg mixture, alternating with oil and water. Add
vanilla, mixing well. Beat with an electric mixer on medium speed for
3 minutes; fold in pecans. Divide batter among 3 greased 5"x3" loaf pans.
Bake at 350 degrees for one hour. Brush hot Glaze over tops of warm loaves.

Glaze:

1/2 c. sugar
1/4 c. water

1 t. vanilla extract

Mix all ingredients together in a saucepan over medium heat. Bring to
a boil; boil for 3 minutes, stirring often.

Use tiered cake stands for bite-size appetizers...
so handy, and they take up less space on the
buffet table than setting out several serving platters.

Pumpkin Cheese Ball

Makes 2 cups

1/2 c. cream cheese, softened
    and divided
8-oz. pkg. shredded mild Cheddar
    cheese
1/4 c. canned pumpkin

1/4 c. pineapple preserves
1/4 t. allspice
1/4 t. nutmeg
1 pretzel rod, broken in half

In a large bowl, combine all ingredients except pretzel rod. Stir until well
blended. Cover and refrigerate for 2 to 3 hours; shape into a ball. Using a
knife, score vertical lines down the sides to resemble a pumpkin. Insert
pretzel rod half in center for pumpkin stem.

Lengths of burlap are so easy to turn into a table runner...
simply cut and fringe the edges! Wonderful for
harvest-time gatherings.

Pumpkin Pie Dip

7-oz. jar marshmallow creme
8-oz. pkg. regular or light cream
    cheese, room temperature
1/2 c. to 3/4 c. canned pumpkin

1 to 2 t. pumpkin pie spice,
    to taste
1 to 3 T. powdered sugar, to taste
vanilla wafers

Combine marshmallow creme, cream cheese and pumpkin in a large bowl. Beat with an electric mixer on medium speed until well combined and smooth. Add spice and powdered sugar in smallest amounts first; stir together. Adjust to taste. For best flavor, cover and refrigerate overnight before serving. Serve with vanilla wafers.

Whip up a jolly Jack-o'-Lantern shake! In a blender, combine 3 scoops vanilla ice cream, 2 tablespoons canned pumpkin, 1/4 cup milk and 1/4 teaspoon pumpkin pie spice. Blend until smooth. Pour into tall glasses and share with a friend.

Smoky Pumpkin Seeds

Makes one cup

1 to 2 T. olive oil
1 c. pumpkin seeds
1 t. garlic salt
1/4 t. chipotle pepper
1/4 t. paprika
1/4 t. smoke-flavored
    cooking sauce

Drizzle an aluminum foil-covered baking sheet with oil. Add pumpkin seeds to baking sheet; sprinkle with remaining ingredients. Stir seeds with a fork until coated in oil and spices. Bake, uncovered, at 350 degrees for about 25 minutes, stirring after 12 minutes. Let cool before serving.

For a yummy lunchbox treat, tuck in a covered container of creamy dip along with some fresh fruit or veggie dippers.

Pumpkin Patch Dip

Makes about 2 cups

8-oz. pkg. cream cheese, softened
3/4 c. canned pumpkin
1 c. finely shredded Cheddar
    cheese
1 T. brown sugar, packed

1/4 t. cinnamon
1/4 t. allspice
1/4 t. nutmeg
assorted snack crackers,
    vegetable slices

Mix all ingredients together except crackers and vegetables in a bowl. Stir until well-combined and smooth. Cover and refrigerate until chilled. Serve with assorted crackers and vegetables.

Share chills & thrills with a monster movie night. Make a big batch of a favorite snack mix, let the kids each invite a special friend and scatter plump cushions on the floor for extra seating. Sure to be fun for everyone!

Dangerously Addictive
Spiced Nut Mix

Makes 6 to 8 servings

1/4 c. butter, sliced
1 c. sugar
1-1/2 t. pumpkin pie spice
1/2 t. cinnamon
1/2 t. allspice

1/2 t. ground ginger
1/2 t. salt
2 c. salted dry-roasted peanuts,
    or a mix of peanuts, whole
    almonds and/or pecan halves

Combine all ingredients in a heavy skillet over medium heat. Cook, stirring constantly, until sugar is melted and golden, coating nuts, about 15 minutes. Spread nuts in a thin layer on aluminum foil-lined rimmed baking sheets. Cool completely; break into clusters. Store in an airtight container.

For crunchy variety in autumn snacking, try Mexican
pumpkin seeds, called "pepitas." They're available
year 'round in the Mexican food section of
most grocery stores.

Goblin Good Snack Mix

Makes about 11 cups

4 c. bite-size crispy cereal squares
4 c. popped kettle corn or regular
    popcorn
1 c. honey-roasted peanuts
1 c. salted roasted pumpkin seeds
1/4 c. butter

6 T. brown sugar, packed
2 T. light corn syrup
1/4 t. vanilla extract
1/4 t. pumpkin pie spice
1 c. candy corn and/or
    candy pumpkins

In a 4-quart microwave-safe bowl, mix cereal, popcorn, peanuts and pumpkin seeds; set aside. In a microwave-safe bowl, combine butter, brown sugar, corn syrup and vanilla. Microwave, uncovered, on high setting for about 2 minutes, until mixture is boiling; stir after one minute. Stir in spice. Pour over cereal mixture and stir until evenly coated. Microwave for 5 minutes, stirring after every minute. Spread on wax paper-lined baking sheets. Let cool for about 15 minutes, stirring occasionally to break up any large pieces. Add candy and toss to mix. Store in an airtight container.

When you rise in the morning,
form a resolution to make the day
a happy one for a fellow creature.

— Sydney Smith

Jack-o'-Latte Coffee

Makes 6 generous servings

5 c. strong brewed coffee
4 c. milk
1/2 c. whipping cream
1/3 c. sugar
1/4 c. canned pumpkin

1 t. vanilla extract
1 t. pumpkin pie spice
Garnish: whipped cream,
    additional pumpkin pie spice

In a 3-quart slow cooker, combine all ingredients except garnish. Whisk until well combined. Cover and cook on high setting for 2 hours, stirring once after one hour. Serve in mugs, topped with a dollop of whipped cream and a sprinkle of spice.

Serve up smoothies and shakes in hollowed-out
mini pumpkins... just for silly fun!

Harvest Hot White Chocolate

Makes 6 to 8 servings

15-oz. can pumpkin
14-oz. can sweetened
   condensed milk
4 c. whole milk
1 t. vanilla extract

1 t. pumpkin pie spice
1-1/4 c. white chocolate chips
Garnish: whipped cream, pumpkin
   pie spice, cinnamon sticks

In a large saucepan, combine pumpkin, milks, vanilla and spice; whisk well. Bring to a simmer over medium heat, stirring frequently. Add chocolate chips; stir until melted. Pour into mugs; garnish with whipped cream, a sprinkle of spice and a cinnamon stick for stirring.

Slide a long length of kitchen twine through the holes in glazed doughnuts, then hang them from tree branches. With hands held behind backs, who can catch and eat a doughnut first?

Marcie's Autumn Tea

Makes about 3 quarts

5 tea bags
1/2 c. sugar
5 c. boiling water
5 c. unsweetened apple juice

2 c. cranberry juice cocktail
1/3 c. lemon juice
1/4 t. pumpkin pie spice
ice cubes

Combine tea bags and sugar in a heat-proof one-gallon pitcher. Add boiling water; let stand for 8 minutes. Discard tea bags. Add juices and spice; stir well until sugar is dissolved. Chill; serve over ice.

Savor warm, sunny Indian summer days on the porch.
Spruce up your outdoor chairs or pull together mismatched
yard-sale finds...it's simple! Spray-paint them all the same
color or use a rainbow of colors just for fun.

Leona's Apple-Carrot Slaw

Makes 4 servings

1/2 c. sweetened dried cranberries
1/2 c. orange juice, divided
2 Granny Smith apples, cored and
    cut into matchsticks
4 carrots, peeled and cut into
    matchsticks

1/4 c. red onion, thinly sliced
1/2 c. pumpkin seed kernels
1/4 c. chopped pecans
3 T. olive oil
pepper to taste

Combine cranberries and 1/4 cup orange juice in a small bowl; set aside. In a separate bowl, toss apples with remaining orange juice; add carrots, onion, pumpkin seeds and pecans. Drain cranberries, reserving the orange juice; add cranberries to apple mixture. Whisk reserved orange juice with olive oil; pour over salad. Season with pepper; toss lightly to coat well. Serve chilled or at room temperature.

There are lots of tasty choices for crisp autumn salads. Start with
cool-weather greens like romaine lettuce, endive, fennel, Swiss
chard and cabbage. Add crunchy apple slices or tender diced pears,
a sprinkling of nuts or seeds and perhaps some crumbled feta or
blue cheese. Drizzle with a fruity vinaigrette...delicious!

Cranberry-Pear Tossed Salad

Makes 4 servings

4 c. arugula lettuce mix
1 pear, cored and sliced
1/2 c. sweetened dried cranberries

1/2 c. pumpkin seeds
1/2 c. raspberry-walnut salad
    dressing, or to taste

Divide lettuce mix among 4 salad plates. Top with pear slices, cranberries and pumpkin seeds. Drizzle with salad dressing. Serve immediately.

There's nothing more cozy than a bowl of warm soup. For extra comfort, warm up oven-safe bowls in a 200-degree oven before filling...the soup (and guests) will stay warmer longer!

October Bisque

Makes 8 servings

1 onion, chopped
1/4 c. butter
4 c. chicken broth
28-oz. can whole tomatoes

2 15-oz. cans pumpkin
2 T. fresh parsley, chopped
2 T. fresh chives, chopped
1 T. sugar

In a large saucepan over medium heat, sauté onion in butter until onion is tender. Add chicken broth and simmer for 15 minutes. Add tomatoes with juice to a blender or food processor;process until smooth. Add tomato mixture and remaining ingredients to broth mixture; heat through.

Everyone loves a picnic and you don't need to head to
the park to have one. Even if you don't have a deck or
a patio, colorful blankets spread on the lawn (or in the
living room!) create excitement for guests.

Pumpkin Chowder

1/2 lb. bacon, diced
2 c. onions, chopped
2 t. curry powder
2 T. all-purpose flour
1-lb. pie pumpkin, peeled,
    seeded and cubed

2 potatoes, peeled and cubed
4 c. chicken broth
1 c. half-and-half
salt and pepper to taste
Garnish: toasted pumpkin seeds,
    sliced green onions

In a stockpot over medium heat, cook bacon for 5 minutes, or until nearly crisp. Partially drain; add onions to remaining drippings and sauté for 10 minutes. Sprinkle with curry powder and flour, stirring until smooth and creamy; cook for about 5 minutes. Add pumpkin, potatoes and chicken broth; simmer until pumpkin and potatoes are tender, about 15 minutes. Pour in half-and-half; season with salt and pepper. Simmer over low heat for 5 minutes; do not boil. Spoon into serving bowls; garnish with pumpkin seeds and onions.

Little sugar pumpkins are sweet
soup bowls...the ideal size!

Pumpkin Patch Soup

2 t. olive oil
1/2 c. raw pumpkin seeds
3 slices thick-cut bacon
1 onion, chopped
1 t. salt
1/2 t. chipotle chili powder

1/2 t. pepper
2 29-oz. cans pumpkin
4 c. chicken broth
3/4 c. apple cider
1/2 c. whipping cream

Heat oil in a small skillet over medium heat. Add pumpkin seeds to oil;
cook and stir until seeds begin to pop, about one minute. Remove seeds
to a bowl and set aside. Add bacon to skillet and cook until crisp. Remove
bacon to a paper towel; crumble and refrigerate. Add onion to drippings in
pan. Sauté until translucent, about 5 minutes. Stir in seasonings. Spoon
onion mixture into a slow cooker. Whisk pumpkin, chicken broth and cider
into onion mixture. Cover and cook on high setting for 4 hours. Whisk in
cream. Top servings with pumpkin seeds and crumbled bacon.

Top bowls of hot soup with popcorn instead of croutons for a crunchy surprise.

Sandra's Creamy Butternut Soup

Makes 4 servings

2 onions, chopped
2 T. butter
1 T. olive oil
15-oz. can pumpkin
1-1/2 lbs. butternut squash,
    peeled and cubed

3 c. chicken broth
2 to 2-1/2 t. salt, divided
1/2 t. pepper
1 c. half-and-half
Optional: shredded Gruyère
    cheese, croutons

In a large saucepan over medium-low heat, sauté onions in butter and oil for 10 minutes. Add pumpkin, squash, chicken broth, 2 teaspoons salt and pepper. Cover and simmer for 20 minutes until squash is very tender. Process mixture until smooth with an immersion blender or in a food processor. Add half-and-half and reheat slowly over low heat; add remaining salt to taste. Top servings with Gruyère cheese and croutons, if desired.

Invite friends over for a Soup Supper on a frosty
winter evening. Everyone can bring their favorite
soup or bread to share...you provide the bowls,
spoons and a crackling fire!

Pumpkin-Wild Rice Soup

Serves 4

6-oz. pkg. long-grain &
   wild rice mix
1 T. butter
1 onion, diced

4 c. chicken broth
1 c. canned pumpkin
1/2 c. whipping cream

Prepare rice mix according to package directions; set aside. Meanwhile, melt butter in a large saucepan over medium heat. Add onion; cook until softened. Stir in chicken broth, pumpkin and cooked rice. Bring to a boil; reduce heat to low. Stir in cream and heat through, about 10 minutes.

If you like toasted pumpkin seeds, try toasting winter squash seeds too! Rinse seeds and pat dry, toss with olive oil to coat, spread on a baking sheet and sprinkle with salt. Bake at 350 degrees for 10 to 15 minutes, until crisp. Yummy!

Pumpkin Patch Stew

Makes 6 to 8 servings

1 onion, finely chopped
1 clove garlic, minced
1 T. dried basil
1 T. olive oil
2 lbs. pork tenderloin, cubed
28-oz. can diced tomatoes
15-oz. can pumpkin
14-1/2 oz. can chicken broth

1/2 c. white wine or chicken broth
1/2 t. salt
1/4 t. pepper
4 potatoes, peeled and cubed
1/2 lb. green beans, trimmed and
    cut into 1-inch pieces
4-inch cinnamon stick

In a stockpot over medium heat, sauté onion, garlic and basil in oil until onion is tender, one to 2 minutes. Add pork cubes; cook for 3 to 4 minutes, until lightly browned. Stir in tomatoes with juice, pumpkin, chicken broth, wine or broth, salt and pepper; bring to a boil. Reduce heat to low; cook, stirring occasionally, for 10 minutes. Add remaining ingredients. Cover and simmer for one hour, or until potatoes are tender. Discard cinnamon stick at serving time.

Keep the week's menu and shopping list right at your fingertips. Criss-cross a bulletin board with tacked-on lengths of wide rick-rack and just slip lists underneath...so handy!

Pumpkin Joes

1-1/2 lbs. ground beef sirloin
1 onion, chopped
12-oz. bottle chili sauce
1/2 c. canned pumpkin
10-3/4 oz. can tomato soup

1 T. pumpkin pie spice
1 t. salt
1 t. pepper
6 to 8 sandwich buns, split

Brown beef with onion in a large skillet over medium heat. Drain; stir in remaining ingredients except buns. Reduce heat; cover and simmer, stirring occasionally, for one hour. To serve, spoon beef mixture onto buns.

As the weather cools, every sofa should have an
inviting throw folded over the back for snuggling!
Why not pull out that afghan Great-Aunt Sophie crocheted
years ago, or a treasured baby quilt that's been outgrown?

Dinner in a Pumpkin

Makes 6 to 8 servings

1 medium pumpkin
1-1/2 c. celery, chopped
1 c. onion, chopped
4-oz. can sliced mushrooms,
    drained
1 T. butter

1 lb. ground beef
10-3/4 oz. can cream of
    chicken soup
4 c. cooked rice
1/2 c. soy sauce
2 T. brown sugar, packed

Cut the top off pumpkin; remove seeds and clean out the inside well. Set aside pumpkin and pumpkin top. In a skillet over medium heat, sauté celery, onion and mushrooms in butter. Remove celery mixture to a large bowl; set aside. Brown beef in the same skillet; drain well. Combine beef and remaining ingredients with celery mixture; stir well. Spoon mixture into pumpkin; replace top. Set pumpkin on a baking sheet. Bake at 350 degrees for one hour. To serve, scoop out some of the inside of the pumpkin along with filling.

Grouped on a table or buffet, a mix of old
and new lanterns greets guests with the
warm glow of candlelight.

Pumpkin-Sausage Penne

Makes 8 servings

16-oz. pkg. penne pasta,
    uncooked
16-oz. pkg. maple-flavored ground
    pork sausage
8-oz. pkg. cream cheese, cubed
2/3 c. grated Parmesan cheese
1/2 c. butter, sliced

1/2 c. milk
1 c. canned pumpkin
1/2 t. cayenne pepper
nutmeg to taste
Optional: additional grated
    Parmesan cheese

Cook pasta according to package directions; drain. Meanwhile, in a skillet, brown sausage over medium heat; drain and set aside. In a large saucepan, combine cream cheese, Parmesan cheese, butter and milk in a large saucepan. Cook over low heat until cream cheese is melted, stirring frequently. Stir in pumpkin and spices; cook until heated through, stirring occasionally. Add cooked pasta and sausage; toss lightly. Serve topped with additional Parmesan cheese, if desired.

Remember to tote along some blankets or folding stools when you go camping...there's nothing like sitting around a glowing campfire stargazing, swapping stories and just savoring time together with friends & family!

Can-Do Ham Dinner

Serves 4 to 6

1 T. oil
2 to 3-lb. canned ham, sliced
1 to 2 16-oz. cans cut yams or
    sweet potatoes, drained

pepper to taste
8-oz. can crushed pineapple,
    drained
1/2 t. pumpkin pie spice

Heat oil in a skillet over medium heat. Add ham slices; heat through. Turn ham over; pour yams over ham. Sprinkle with pepper. Top with pineapple; sprinkle with spice. Reduce heat to medium-low and simmer until pineapple is caramelized, about 15 minutes.

The leaves fall, the wind blows,
and the farm country slowly changes
from the summer cottons into its winter wools.

-Henry Beston

Ruby Chicken

Makes 8 servings

2 lbs. boneless, skinless chicken
    breasts, cubed
1 onion, chopped
12-oz. can frozen orange juice
    concentrate, thawed
zest of 1 orange
1 orange, chopped

12-oz. pkg. fresh cranberries
1 c. sugar
2 T. oil
2 t. salt
1 t. pumpkin pie spice
cooked rice

Add all ingredients except rice to a slow cooker. Cover and cook on low setting for 6 to 8 hours, until chicken juices run clear. Serve chicken and sauce from slow cooker over cooked rice.

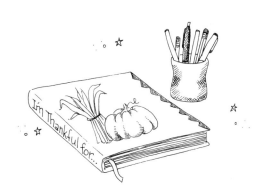

Start a new Thanksgiving tradition. Decorate a blank book
and invite everyone to write what they're thankful for.
The tradition will become even more meaningful as
it's continued, year after year.

Farmstead Pumpkin Casserole *Makes 6 to 8 servings*

15-oz. can pumpkin
14-oz. can sweetened condensed
   milk
1/4 c. butter, melted

1/2 c. sugar
4 eggs, beaten
2 t. cinnamon

Combine all ingredients in a bowl; mix well. Pour into a lightly greased 2-quart casserole dish. Bake, uncovered, at 325 degrees for 45 minutes, or until set.

Short on chairs for a backyard gathering? Arrange hay bales for super easy, country-style seating.

Pumpkin Hollow Surprise

Makes 8 to 12 servings

5 to 7-lb. pie pumpkin
1 to 2 T. oil
2/3 c. raisins, golden raisins
    or currants
2/3 c. sweetened dried cranberries

4 apples, cored and chopped
2/3 c. chopped pecans or walnuts
1 t. pumpkin pie spice
1/2 to 1 c. brown sugar, packed

Cut the top from the pumpkin; scoop out seeds. Place pumpkin on a baking sheet covered with aluminum foil. Rub oil lightly over the outside of pumpkin and top; set aside. In a large bowl, combine fruit and nuts; add spice and brown sugar. Depending upon the size of pumpkin, more or less fruit may be needed to fill pumpkin. Spoon fruit mixture into pumpkin; set top next to it on baking sheet. Bake at 325 degrees for about 30 to 45 minutes, until apples are tender. To serve, scoop out some of the inside of pumpkin; serve alongside the fruit mixture.

Make a cornhusk wreath! Remove the husks from dried ears of corn and fold them in half. Wrap ends with thin wire and insert the wires into a straw wreath, covering all sides. Add dried yarrow, bittersweet and wheat for a wonderful welcome-to-fall decoration.

Simmered Autumn Applesauce

Makes 6 servings

8 apples, several different
    varieties, peeled, cored
    and cubed
1 c. water

1/2 c. brown sugar, packed
1 t. cinnamon
1/2 t. pumpkin pie spice

Add all ingredients to a slow cooker; stir. Cover and cook on low setting for 6 to 8 hours. Mash apples with the back of a spoon; stir again. Let cool slightly before serving.

Create a fun fall centerpiece in a snap! Hot-glue ears of
mini Indian corn around a terra cotta pot and set
a vase of orange or yellow mums in the center.

Buttery Acorn Squash

3/4 c. brown sugar, packed
2 t. pumpkin pie spice
2 acorn squash, halved
   and seeded

3/4 c. raisins
1/4 c. butter, sliced
1/2 c. water

In a small bowl, combine brown sugar and spice; spoon into squash halves. Sprinkle with raisins; dot with butter. Wrap each squash half separately in heavy-duty aluminum foil; seal tightly. Add water to a slow cooker. Place squash in slow cooker, cut-side up, stacking packets if necessary. Cover and cook on high setting for 4 hours, or until squash is tender. Open packets carefully to allow steam to escape.

As autumn evenings turn dark, light a candle
or two at the family dinner table. It'll make an
ordinary meal seem special!

Blue-Ribbon Pumpkin Roll

Serves 10 to 12

2/3 c. canned pumpkin
3 eggs, beaten
1 c. sugar
3/4 c. all-purpose flour
1 t. baking soda

1 t. cinnamon
1 c. plus 3 T. powdered sugar, divided
8-oz. pkg. cream cheese, softened
1 t. vanilla extract

In a large bowl, blend together pumpkin, eggs and sugar; set aside. In a separate bowl, combine flour, baking soda and cinnamon; fold into pumpkin mixture. Line a 15"x10" jelly-roll pan with parchment paper. Grease and flour the paper; spread batter into pan. Bake at 350 degrees for 15 minutes. Sprinkle 3 tablespoons powdered sugar on a tea towel; turn out warm cake onto towel. Carefully peel off parchment paper. Starting at narrow end, roll up cake and towel together; cool completely on a wire rack, seam-side down. Blend cream cheese, remaining powdered sugar and vanilla until smooth. Unroll cake; spread with cream cheese mixture and re-roll, removing towel as you roll. Place on a serving plate, seam-side down. Cover and chill at least 2 hours before slicing.

Looking for a new no-mess way to decorate Jack-o'-Lanterns?
Try duct tape! It comes in lots of fun colors and is super-easy
to cut into shapes...great for kids to craft with. Later, the
uncut pumpkin can even be re-purposed for pies.

Gingersnap Pumpkin Pie

Serves 8

15-oz. can pumpkin
14-oz. can sweetened
   condensed milk
2 eggs, beaten

1/8 t. salt
2 T. plus 1/2 t. pumpkin pie
   spice, divided

In a large bowl, blend pumpkin and condensed milk. Add eggs, salt and
2 tablespoons spice; mix well. Pour into Gingersnap Crust; sprinkle with
remaining spice. Bake at 425 degrees for 15 minutes. Cover edges of
crust with strips of aluminum foil, if browning too fast. Reduce oven
to 350 degrees and bake for another 35 minutes, or until set. Cool
before slicing.

Gingersnap Crust:

1-1/2 c. gingersnaps, crushed
Optional: 2 T. hazelnuts, crushed

3/4 c. butter, melted

Toss cookie crumbs and nuts, if using, with butter. Press into the bottom
and up the sides of a 9" pie plate.

One of the best ways to give thanks is to help someone else.
Volunteer, lend a neighbor a hand, leave a surprise on someone's
doorstep...there are lots of thoughtful ways to show you care.

Pumpkin Custard Crunch

Makes 9 to 12 servings

29-oz. can pumpkin
3 eggs, beaten
2 t. pumpkin pie spice
1 t. cinnamon

14-oz. can sweetened
    condensed milk
1 c. milk
2 t. vanilla extract

In a large bowl, stir together pumpkin, eggs and spices well; stir in milks and vanilla. Pour into a greased 13"x9" baking pan; spoon Crunch Topping over pumpkin mixture. Bake at 350 degrees for 45 to 60 minutes, until a knife tip comes out clean. Watch carefully so that topping doesn't burn. Serve warm.

Crunch Topping:

3 c. quick-cooking oats, uncooked
1 c. brown sugar, packed
1 c. all-purpose flour

1 t. cinnamon
1 c. walnuts or pecans, crushed
1 c. butter, melted

Stir together oats, brown sugar, flour, cinnamon and nuts. Add melted butter; toss to mix.

Wow guests with a pumpkin-shaped cake. Place one Bundt® cake upside-down on a cake stand. Place a second cake right-side up on top and secure with frosting. Ice with orange frosting.

Perfect Pumpkin-Apple Cake

Serves 8

1/2 c. butter, softened
1-1/2 c. brown sugar, packed
1 c. canned pumpkin
3 eggs
2 c. all-purpose flour
2 t. baking powder
1/4 t. baking soda

1 t. cinnamon
1/4 t. salt
Optional: chopped walnuts or
    pecans to taste
21-oz. can apple pie filling
12-oz. container frozen whipped
    topping, thawed

In a large bowl, beat together butter and brown sugar with an electric mixer on low speed until well mixed. Beat in pumpkin and eggs until blended; set aside. In a separate bowl, sift together flour, baking powder, baking soda, cinnamon and salt. Slowly add flour mixture to butter mixture; beat for 2 minutes. Fold in nuts, if using. Spoon pie filling into a slow cooker; pour batter over pie filling. Cover and cook on high setting for 1-1/2 to 2 hours, until a toothpick tests clean. Garnish servings with a dollop of whipped topping.

Greet your guests with a whimsical pumpkin tower
on the front porch. Arrange pumpkins and squash
in graduated sizes in a stack, using skewers to
hold them in place. Clever!

Pumpkin Mallow Pie

Makes 2 pies, 8 servings each

15-oz. can pumpkin
2 10-oz. pkgs. mini
    marshmallows
1 t. cinnamon

1 pt. whipping cream
2 9-inch graham cracker
    pie crusts

In a heavy saucepan over low heat, combine pumpkin, marshmallows and
cinnamon; cook and stir until marshmallows are melted. Remove from
heat; cover and chill thoroughly. Pour whipping cream into a deep bowl.
Beat with an electric mixer on high speed until soft peaks form; set aside.
Beat chilled pumpkin mixture until fluffy; fold in whipped cream. Divide
and spread evenly into pie crusts; chill until firm.

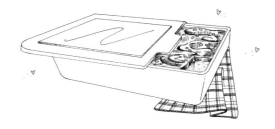

If you see a vintage cake pan with its own slide-on lid at a tag sale, snap it up! It's indispensable for toting cakes and bar cookies to picnics and potlucks.

Crustless Pumpkin Pie

Makes 8 to 10 servings

4 eggs, beaten
15-oz. can pumpkin
12-oz. can evaporated milk
1-1/2 c. sugar
2 t. pumpkin pie spice
1 t. salt

18-1/2 oz. pkg. yellow cake mix
1 c. chopped pecans or walnuts
1 c. butter, melted
Optional: whipped topping,
   chopped nuts, cinnamon

In a large bowl, combine eggs, pumpkin, evaporated milk, sugar, spice and salt. Mix well; pour into an ungreased 13"x9" baking pan. Sprinkle dry cake mix and nuts over top. Drizzle with butter; do not stir. Bake at 350 degrees for 45 minutes to one hour, testing for doneness with a toothpick. Serve topped with whipped topping, sprinkled with nuts and cinnamon.

Bread pudding is a scrumptious way to use up day-old bread.
Try French bread, raisin bread or even leftover cinnamon
buns or doughnuts for an extra-tasty dessert!

Pumpkin Bread Pudding

Makes 8 servings

3 c. bread, cubed
1/4 c. butter, melted
29-oz. can pumpkin
2 c. 2% reduced-fat milk
4 eggs, beaten

1/4 c. sugar
1 t. vanilla extract
1 t. cinnamon
1 t. nutmeg

Coat the inside of a slow cooker with non-stick vegetable spray. Combine bread and melted butter in a bowl; toss to coat. Add enough bread cubes to line slow cooker; set aside. In a separate bowl, beat together remaining ingredients; pour over bread cubes. Cover and cook on high setting for one hour, or on low setting for 3 to 4 hours, until set.

Make a yummy ice cream pie in a jiffy. Pat a tube
of refrigerated cookie dough into a pie plate. Chill for
30 minutes, then bake as package directs. Let cool,
then fill with spoonfuls of ice cream...yum!

Pumpkin-Gingersnap Ice Cream *Makes 6 to 8 servings*

14-oz. container vanilla
   ice cream, softened
15-oz. can pumpkin
1 sleeve gingersnap cookies,
   crushed

Optional: whipped cream,
   additional gingersnaps,
   candy corn

In a large bowl, combine ice cream and pumpkin; blend well by hand. Stir in crushed cookies. Cover and freeze. If desired, garnish scoops of ice cream with a dollop of whipped cream, a gingersnap cookie and several pieces of candy corn.

A loaf of homemade bread is always a welcome gift!
Make sure it stays fresh and tasty...let the bread cool
completely before wrapping well in plastic wrap or aluminum foil.

Chocolate-Pumpkin Bread

Makes 12 to 15 servings

1 to 2 T. butter, softened
1-2/3 c. all-purpose flour
1/4 t. baking powder
1 t. baking soda
1 T. pumpkin pie spice
3/4 t. salt
2 eggs, beaten

1-1/2 c. sugar
1/2 c. oil
1 c. canned pumpkin
1/2 c. water
1 c. semi-sweet chocolate chips
Optional: 1/2 c. toasted nuts

Choose a loaf pan or metal coffee can that fits into your slow cooker. Generously coat pan with butter; set aside. In a bowl, mix flour, baking powder, baking soda, spice and salt. In a separate large bowl, beat together eggs, sugar and oil; beat in pumpkin and water. Add flour mixture to egg mixture, mixing well; stir in chocolate chips and nuts, if using. Spoon batter into pan; place in slow cooker. Cover and cook on high setting for 3 to 4 hours, until a toothpick inserted in center comes out clean. Cool bread in pan 15 minutes. Turn out onto a wire rack; cool completely. This bread freezes well.

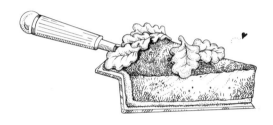

Beautify your pie! Roll out extra pie crust, cut out tiny
fall leaves with cookie cutters and place them all along
the rim of the pie plate before baking.

Traditional Pumpkin Pie *Makes 2 pies, 8 servings each*

2 9-inch pie crusts, unbaked
4 eggs
3 c. canned pumpkin
3-1/3 c. evaporated milk
1-1/2 c. sugar

1 t. salt
2 t. cinnamon
1 t. ground ginger
1/2 t. ground cloves
Garnish: whipped cream

Arrange each pie crust in a 9" pie plate; pinch the edges. Pierce the bottom and sides of crusts with a fork and set aside. In a large bowl, combine remaining ingredients except garnish; whisk well. Divide evenly between the 2 crusts. Bake at 425 degrees for 15 minutes. Turn oven down to 350 degrees; bake for an additional 45 minutes. If rims of crusts are browning too quickly while baking, cover with strips of aluminum foil. Let cool before cutting. Garnish individual slices with whipped cream.

To keep the top of your Marbled Pumpkin Cheesecake
from cracking, place a shallow pan of water on the
lower rack of the oven while it bakes.

Marbled Pumpkin Cheesecake

Serves 6 to 8

3/4 c. gingersnaps, crushed
3/4 c. graham crackers, crushed
1-1/4 c. sugar, divided
1/4 c. butter, melted
2 8-oz. pkgs. cream cheese,
    softened

4 eggs
15-oz. can pumpkin
1/2 t. cinnamon
1/4 t. ground ginger
1/4 t. nutmeg

In a bowl, combine gingersnap and graham cracker crumbs, 1/4 cup sugar and butter. Mix well; press into the bottom of a 9" springform pan. Bake at 350 degrees for 5 minutes; set aside. In another bowl, beat cream cheese with an electric mixer on medium speed until smooth. Gradually add remaining sugar; beat until light. Add eggs, one at a time, beating well after each. Transfer 1-1/2 cups cream cheese mixture to a separate bowl; blend in pumpkin and spices. Pour half of pumpkin mixture into baked crumb crust. Top with half of cream cheese mixture. Repeat layers, using remaining pumpkin and cream cheese mixtures. Using a table knife, cut through layers with an uplifting motion in 4 or 5 places to create a marbled effect. Bake at 350 degrees for 45 minutes; do not open oven door. When baked, turn off oven and let cheesecake stand for one hour. Remove and chill before serving.

Serve hot spiced coffee with sweet autumn treats.
Simply add 3/4 teaspoon pumpkin pie spice to
1/2 cup ground coffee and brew as usual.

Gail's Pumpkin Bars

Makes 1-1/2 to 2 dozen

4 eggs, beaten
1 c. oil
2 c. sugar
15-oz. can pumpkin
2 c. all-purpose flour
2 t. baking powder

1 t. baking soda
1/2 t. salt
2 t. cinnamon
1/2 t. ground ginger
1/2 t. nutmeg
1/2 t. ground cloves

Whisk together eggs, oil, sugar and pumpkin in a large bowl. Add remaining ingredients and mix well. Pour into a greased and floured 18"x12" jelly-roll pan. Bake at 350 degrees for 30 to 40 minutes, until a toothpick comes out clean. Let cool; frost with Cream Cheese Frosting and cut into bars.

Cream Cheese Frosting:

8-oz. pkg. cream cheese, softened
6 T. butter, softened
1 T. milk

1 t. vanilla extract
4 c. powdered sugar

Beat together cream cheese, butter, milk and vanilla. Gradually stir in powdered sugar to a spreading consistency.

Fall mums come in glorious shades of red, yellow and orange...
you can't have too many! Tuck pots into hollowed-out
pumpkins to march up the porch steps.

Pumpkin Spice & Chocolate Bars

Makes 20

2 eggs, beaten
1/2 c. oil
18-1/2 oz. pkg. yellow cake mix
1 t. pumpkin pie spice

1-1/2 c. semi-sweet chocolate
  chips
1/2 c. chopped nuts

In a bowl, whisk together eggs and oil. Stir in dry cake mix and spice until well blended. Fold in chocolate chips and nuts. Spread batter in a greased 13"x9" baking pan. Bake at 350 degrees for 28 to 30 minutes. Cool completely; cut into bars.

Save the sprinkles! Before adding candy sprinkles to cookies, cover the table with a length of wax paper. Return any excess sprinkles to their jar by simply folding the paper in half, gently shaking sprinkles to one side and sliding them into the jar.

Mom's Pumpkin Brownies

Makes 8 to 10

4 eggs, room temperature
2 c. sugar
1 c. butter, melted and
    slightly cooled
1 c. canned pumpkin
1 t. vanilla extract

1-1/2 c. all-purpose flour
1-1/2 t. pumpkin pie spice
1/2 t. cinnamon
Garnish: vanilla or cream
    cheese frosting

In a large bowl, beat eggs well with an electric mixer on medium speed.
Beat in sugar, butter, pumpkin and vanilla on medium speed. Add flour
and spices; beat on low speed until smooth. Spread batter in a lightly
greased 9"x9" baking pan. Bake at 350 degrees for 40 minutes. Cool;
frost as desired and cut into squares.

Keep cookies soft and moist. Tuck a slice of bread into the storage bag or cookie jar.

Pumpkin-Chocolate Chip Cookies

Makes 2 dozen

16-1/2 oz. pkg. spice cake mix
15-oz. can pumpkin

1 c. semi-sweet chocolate chips

In a bowl, combine dry cake mix, pumpkin and chocolate chips; mix well together. Scoop heaping tablespoonfuls of dough onto greased baking sheets. Bake at 350 degrees for 10 to 12 minutes, just until firm. Remove cookies to a wire rack and cool.

A terrific party favor... jumbo cookies tucked into paper CD envelopes from the office supply store. Decorate the envelopes with stickers or rubber stamps. Your guests will thank you!

Grandma Ila's Pumpkin Cookies *Makes 2 to 3 dozen*

1 c. shortening
1 c. sugar
1 c. canned pumpkin
1 egg, beaten
2 t. vanilla extract, divided
2 c. all-purpose flour
1 t. baking powder

1 t. baking soda
1/2 t. salt
1 t. cinnamon
8-oz. pkg. cream cheese, softened
1/4 c. butter, softened
2 c. powdered sugar

Blend together shortening, sugar, pumpkin and egg in a large bowl; stir in one teaspoon vanilla. In a separate bowl, combine flour, baking powder, baking soda, salt and cinnamon. Gradually beat flour mixture into pumpkin mixture. Drop by rounded tablespoonfuls onto greased baking sheets. Bake at 350 degrees for 12 to 15 minutes; cool completely on wire racks. In another bowl, blend together cream cheese and butter; stir in remaining vanilla. Gradually beat in powdered sugar until fluffy. Spread cookies with frosting.

When the temperature is dropping, treat yourself to a cup of warm mulled cider. Heat a mug of cider to boiling, add an orange spice teabag and let stand several minutes. Mmm!

Pumpkin-Oat Scotchies

Makes 3 dozen

2 c. old-fashioned oats, uncooked
1 c. all-purpose flour
3/4 c. brown sugar, packed
1/2 c. butterscotch chips
1 t. baking soda
1/2 t. salt
1/2 t. pumpkin pie spice
1/2 t. cinnamon
3/4 c. butter, softened
1/2 c. sugar
1 egg, beaten
1/2 c. canned pumpkin
1 t. vanilla extract

In a bowl, combine oats, flour, brown sugar, butterscotch chips, baking soda, salt and spices. Mix well and set aside. In a large bowl, blend butter and sugar together. Add egg, pumpkin and vanilla; stir well. Add oat mixture to butter mixture; mix well. Scoop dough into one-inch balls. Place on ungreased baking sheets, 2 inches apart. Bake at 350 degrees for 10 minutes. Cool on wire racks.

Dress up your fall dinner table with leaf-printed placemats. Brush acrylic craft paint over the back of a leaf and press onto a large piece of paper. Repeat with more leaves to create a border or overall design. When dry, protect the placemat with clear self-stick plastic.

Pumpkin Whoopie Pies

Makes 15

1 c. canned pumpkin
1/3 c. butter, softened
18-1/2 oz. pkg. spice cake mix

2 eggs, beaten
1/2 c. milk

In a large bowl, with an electric mixer on medium speed, beat pumpkin and butter together until smooth. Add dry cake mix, eggs and milk. Beat on low speed until combined; increase speed to medium speed and beat for one minute. Drop by heaping tablespoonfuls, 3 inches apart, onto parchment paper-lined baking sheets. Bake at 375 degrees for about 15 minutes, until set and edges are lightly golden. Carefully remove cookies to a wire rack; cool. Spread flat sides of half of cookies with 2-1/2 tablespoons Marshmallow Filling; top with remaining cookies. Keep chilled.

Marshmallow Filling:

8-oz. pkg. cream cheese, softened
1/2 c. butter, softened
1-1/2 c. marshmallow creme
1 t. vanilla extract

1/2 t. cinnamon
1/2 t. nutmeg
2 c. powdered sugar

Blend together cream cheese and butter until smooth. Add remaining ingredients; beat until well combined.

INDEX

INDEX

Our Story

Back in 1984, we were next-door neighbors raising our families in the little town of Delaware, Ohio. Two moms with small children, we were looking for a way to do what we loved and stay home with the kids too. We had always shared a love of home cooking and making memories with family & friends and so, after many a conversation over the backyard fence, **Gooseberry Patch** was born.

We put together our first catalog at our kitchen tables, enlisting the help of our loved ones wherever we could. From that very first mailing, we found an immediate connection with many of our customers and it wasn't long before we began receiving letters, photos and recipes from these new friends. In 1992, we put together our very first cookbook, compiled from hundreds of these recipes and, the rest, as they say, is history.

Hard to believe it's been over 35 years since those kitchen-table days! From that original little **Gooseberry Patch** family, we've grown to include an amazing group of creative folks who love cooking, decorating and creating as much as we do. Today, we're best known for our homestyle, family-friendly cookbooks, now recognized as national bestsellers.

One thing's for sure, we couldn't have done it without our friends all across the country. Each year, we're honored to turn thousands of your recipes into our collectible cookbooks. Our hope is that each book captures the stories and heart of all of you who have shared with us. Whether you've been with us since the beginning or are just discovering us, welcome to the **Gooseberry Patch** family!

Visit our website anytime
www.gooseberrypatch.com

Email

1·800·854·6673

Jo Ann & Vickie